WELCOME

Liverpool Heartbeat is proud to present this fabulous comic book retelling the story of Her Majesty, Queen Elizabeth II, to celebrate her Platinum Jubilee after 70 years of service to our nation.

Liverpool Heartbeat is also celebrating its own 20th anniversary this year of working alongside the young people of Merseyside in the fields of athletics and literacy.

Tim Quinn
Editor

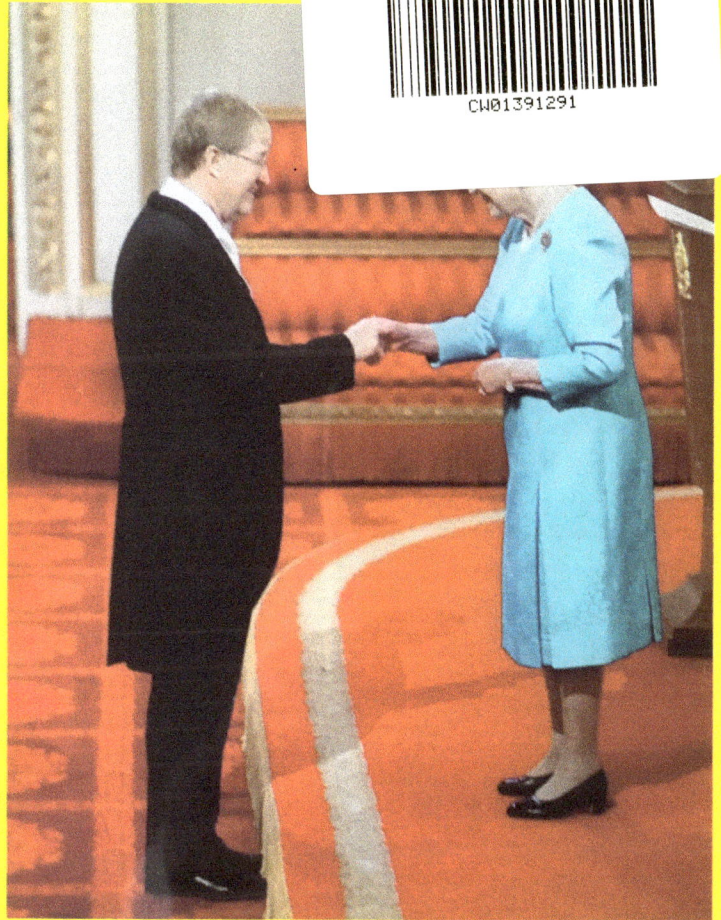

Liverpool Heartbeat MD, Robin Baynes, receiving his MBE from the Queen.

Published 2022
First Edition
PHOENIX PRESS LTD
A New Haven Publishing imprint
www.newhavenpublishingltd.com
phoenixpressltd@gmail.com

PHOENIX
— PRESS —

BUCKINGHAM PALACE, LONDON. HOME OF THE ROYAL FAMILY.....

TODAY IS A SPECIAL DAY FOR THIS MAN....ROBIN BAYNES, HEAD OF THE LIVERPOOL HEARTBEAT CHARITY.

CAN'T BELIEVE I'M HERE.

IT'S A LONG WAY FROM MY LIVERPOOL ROOTS.

FOR THE CHARITABLE WORK HE HAS DONE OVER THE YEARS, ROBIN IS HERE TO RECEIVE A SPECIAL HONOUR...

FOLLOW ME, MR BAYNES.

IT GIVES ME GREAT PLEASURE TO MAKE YOU A MEMBER OF THE BRITISH EMPIRE BY PRESENTING YOU WITH AN MBE.

LATER....

WHAT AN HONOUR AND WHAT AN AMAZING WOMAN. AND WHAT AN INCREDIBLE LIFE STORY SHE HAS TO TELL.....

THE QUEEN'S LIFE BEGAN AT 2:40AM ON 21ST APRIL 1926. HER PROUD PARENTS WERE THE DUKE AND DUCHESS OF YORK, WHO LATER BECAME KING GEORGE VI AND QUEEN ELIZABETH (THE QUEEN MOTHER).

SPLAT!

HA HA HA HA

HA HA HA HA HA HA

THE 1920'S WERE KNOWN AS THE ROARING TWENTIES AS PEOPLE WANTED TO HAVE FUN AFTER THE HARDSHIPS OF THE FIRST WORLD WAR.

LITTLE ELIZABETH, KNOWN AS LILLIBET (BECAUSE THAT'S HOW SHE PRONOUNCED HER NAME AT A YOUNG AGE), ENJOYED MOVIE STARS SUCH AS CHARLIE CHAPLIN AND THE WEEKLY COMIC BOOKS OF THE DAY.

A LOVELY FREE TOY INSIDE!

Tiny

TINY TOTS

TigerTim's ANNUAL

Jolly Christmas Cards to Send to Your Friends

THE CHICKS' OWN 2'

Rupert the Chick's Christ-mas Pud-ding—don't you

YOUNG ELIZABETH ALSO LOVED LISTENING IN TO EARLY RADIO SHOWS ON A DEVICE KNOWN AS THE CAT'S WHISKER.

ELIZABETH PROVED TO BE QUITE ATHLETIC AS A CHILD. ALONG WITH HER YOUNGER SISTER MARGARET SHE SOON BECAME A SKILLED HORSE RIDER. THIS TURNED OUT TO BE A LIFETIME PASTIME.

AFTER THE ABDICATION OF HIS BROTHER EDWARD, ELIZABETH'S FATHER WAS CROWNED KING GEORGE VI IN 1937.

THIS MEANT THAT THE CHILD ELIZABETH WAS SET ON COURSE TO BECOME THE FUTURE QUEEN.

WHILE BRITAIN CELEBRATED THE NEW KING, OVER IN GERMANY A WORLD SHAKING CATASTROPHE WAS IN THE MAKING WITH THE RISE OF ONE MAN AND HIS DIABOLICAL POLITICAL PARTY:
ADOLF HITLER AND THE NAZI PARTY.

AND ON 3RD SEPTEMBER 1939, WORLD WAR 2 STARTED.

READ ALL ABOUT IT!!

PRINCESS ELIZABETH AND HER SISTER MARGARET HELPED KEEP THE PUBLIC SPIRITS HIGH THROUGHOUT THE WAR YEARS WITH REGULAR RADIO BROADCASTS TO THE NATION.

WAR DECLARED!

AT THE AGE OF 19, PRINCESS ELIZABETH JOINED THE AUXILIARY TERRITORIAL SERVICE (ATS). AFTER JOINING, SHE TRAINED AS A DRIVER AND MECHANIC WITH THE RANK OF SECOND SUBALTERN. FIVE MONTHS LATER SHE WAS PROMOTED TO JUNIOR COMMANDER, WHICH WAS THE EQUIVALENT OF CAPTAIN.

AFTER PASSING THE MILITARY DRIVING TEST, ELIZABETH BECAME A DRIVER FOR THE SECOND SUBALTERN WINDSOR UNIT. SHE BECAME THE FIRST FEMALE MEMBER OF THE ROYAL FAMILY TO SERVE IN THE ARMED FORCES AND IS THE ONLY LIVING HEAD OF STATE TO HAVE SERVED IN THE SECOND WORLD WAR.

THE ROYAL FAMILY WERE TAKING TEA IN A DRAWING ROOM OF BUCKINGHAM PALACE ON THE MORNING OF 13 SEPTEMBER 1940...

...WHEN A GERMAN BOMBER PLANE MADE THE PALACE A TARGET FOR THE LUFTWAFFE.

THE ATTACK LEFT THREE PALACE STAFF INJURED BUT THE ROYAL FAMILY ESCAPED UNHARMED.

THE QUEEN MOTHER RESPONDED TO THE ATTACK IN A RADIO BROADCAST...

THE CHILDREN WILL NOT LEAVE UNLESS I DO. I SHALL NOT LEAVE UNLESS THEIR FATHER DOES, AND THE KING WILL NOT LEAVE THE COUNTRY IN ANY CIRCUMSTANCES WHATSOEVER.

BBC

During the Blitz, the Royal Family visited bombed areas to see the damage caused by enemy air raids. On these visits, the Queen took a keen interest in what was being done to help people who had lost their homes. After Buckingham Palace was bombed on 13 September 1940, she said she felt she could 'look the East End in the face'.

ELIZABETH AND HER FUTURE HUSBAND WERE INTRODUCED AT THE WEDDING OF PRINCE PHILIP'S COUSIN, PRINCESS MARINA, TO PRINCE GEORGE, DUKE OF KENT BACK IN 1934. HE WAS 13 YEARS OLD, WHILE THE THEN PRINCESS ELIZABETH WAS AGED EIGHT. THE COUPLE MET AGAIN FIVE YEARS LATER AT DARTMOUTH ROYAL NAVAL COLLEGE.

PHILIP WAS A PRINCE OF GREECE. THROUGH THE WAR YEARS ROMANCE FLOURISHED WITH ELIZABETH AND PHILIP.

THE WEDDING OF PRINCESS ELIZABETH AND PHILIP MOUNTBATTEN TOOK PLACE ON THURSDAY 20th NOVEMBER 1947 AT WESTMINSTER ABBEY IN LONDON, UNITED KINGDOM. THE BRIDE WAS THE ELDER DAUGHTER OF KING GEORGE VI AND HEIR PRESUMPTIVE TO THE BRITISH THRONE. THE GROOM WAS A FORMER GREEK AND DANISH PRINCE.

ELIZABETH II ACCEDED TO THE THRONE AT THE AGE OF 25 UPON THE DEATH OF HER FATHER, GEORGE VI, ON 6 FEBRUARY 1952, BEING PROCLAIMED QUEEN BY HER PRIVY AND EXECUTIVE COUNCILS SHORTLY AFTERWARDS.

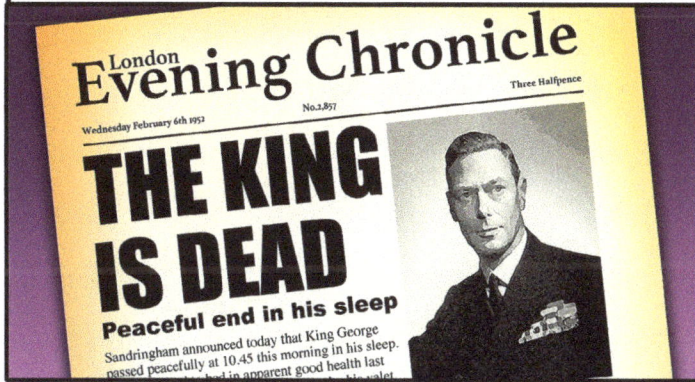

London Evening Chronicle

Wednesday February 6th 1952   No.3,857   Three Halfpence

THE KING IS DEAD

Peaceful end in his sleep

Sandringham announced today that King George passed peacefully at 10.45 this morning in his sleep. ... in apparent good health last ... valet

THE WHOLE COUNTRY PREPARED TO CELEBRATE WITH STREET PARTIES ON THE DAY OF THE CORONATION.

THE CORONATION OF QUEEN ELIZABETH ii, BROADCAST LIVE ON 2 JUNE 1953, WAS THE EVENT THAT DID MORE THAN ANY OTHER TO MAKE TELEVISION A MAINSTREAM MEDIUM. TV AERIALS WERE ERECTED ACROSS THE COUNTRY TO RECEIVE THE TV BROADCAST.

MORE THAN 20 MILLION PEOPLE WATCHED THE SERVICE ON TELEVISION, OUTNUMBERING THE RADIO AUDIENCE FOR THE FIRST TIME. FAMILY AND FRIENDS GATHERED ROUND EACH TELEVISION SET.

9

THE CROWDS TURNED OUT IN THEIR THOUSANDS TO WAVE ALONG THE PROCESSION ROUTE AS ELIZABETH MADE HER WAY TO WESTMINSTER ABBEY IN THE GOLD STATE COACH.

EXTENDED ROUTE

IT WAS COMPLETED IN 1762. THIS COACH HAS BEEN USED AT THE CORONATION OF EVERY BRITISH MONARCH SINCE GEORGE IV

THE PROCESSION AND THE CORONATION WERE BROADCAST THROUGHOUT THE WORLD ON TV FOR THE FIRST TIME. THAT WEEK'S RADIO TIMES MAGAZINE HOLDS THE RECORD FOR MOST COPIES PRINTED OF A SINGLE EDITION OF ANY WEEKLY PUBLICATION- OVER 9,000,000

RADIO TIMES
EⅡR
1953
CORONATION NUMBER

COMMISSIONED IN 1760 BY KING GEORGE III, IT WAS BUILT IN THE LONDON WORKSHOPS OF SAMUEL BUTLER. IT WAS COMMISSIONED FOR £7,562 (£1.5 MILLION = US$1.98 MILLION TODAY).

WESTMINSTER ABBEY HAS BEEN THE SETTING FOR EVERY CORONATION SINCE 1066. BEFORE THE ABBEY WAS BUILT, CORONATIONS WERE CARRIED OUT WHEREVER WAS CONVENIENT, TAKING PLACE IN BATH, OXFORD AND CANTERBURY.

QUEEN ELIZABETH II WAS CROWNED ON 2 JUNE, 1953. HER MAJESTY WAS THE THIRTY-NINTH SOVEREIGN TO BE CROWNED AT WESTMINSTER ABBEY.

QUEEN ELIZABETH II IS THE SIXTH QUEEN TO HAVE BEEN CROWNED IN WESTMINSTER ABBEY. THE FIRST WAS QUEEN MARY I, WHO WAS CROWNED ON 1 OCTOBER, 1553.

NIGEL PARKINSON H.H.

11

On the 14th November 1948, Prince Charles was born to the royal couple. This was followed by Princess Anne's birth on 15th August 1950.

Elizabeth and Philip would have two more children in the following years: Prince Andrew on 19th February 1960 and Prince Edward on 10th March 1964.

The Queen has owned over thirty corgis since her accession in 1952. The Queen herself is credited with creating the dorgi – a dachshund-corgi mix.

The Queen is a keen football supporter with her favourite team being Arsenal.

ENG 4 2 GER ANY W.

The 1966 FIFA World Cup Final was a football match played at Wembley Stadium, London, on 30 July 1966 to determine the winner of the 1966 FIFA World Cup, the eighth FIFA World Cup.

Queen Elizabeth II presented England captain Bobby Moore with the World Cup trophy after England defeated West Germany 4-2.

WINSTON CHURCHILL
1951-1955

ANTHONY EDEN
1955-1957

HAROLD MACMILLAN
1957-1963

ALEC DOUGLAS-HOME
1963-1964

BORIS JOHNSON
2019-present

HAROLD WILSON
1964-1970
1974-1976

THERESA MAY
2016-2019

EDWARD HEATH
1970-1974

DAVID CAMERON
2010-2016

JAMES CALLAGHAN
1976-1979

GORDON BROWN
2007-2010

TONY BLAIR
1997-2007

JOHN MAJOR
1990-1997

MARGARET THATCHER
1979-1990

THE QUEEN'S TRAVELS HAVE TAKEN HER TO 110 COUNTRIES ACROSS SIX CONTINENTS, AND SHE'S STILL GOING STRONG. HER MAJESTY IS THE MOST TRAVELLED MONARCH IN THE WORLD. DESPITE HER ADVANCING AGE, THE QUEEN STILL MAKES STATE VISITS TO IMPORTANT BRITISH ALLIES — WITH TRIPS TO IRELAND, FRANCE AND GERMANY TAKING PLACE IN RECENT YEARS. HER PREFERRED MODE OF TRANSPORT IS EITHER ON THE RAF VOYAGER PLANE OR THE ROYAL YACHT BRITANNIA, WHICH IS DESCRIBED AS A FLOATING PALACE.

ARCTIC OCEAN

ASIA

INDIAN OCEAN

AUSTRALIA →

GREENLAND

EUROPE

AFRICA

ATLANTIC OCEAN

RAF Voyager

NORTH AMERICA

HOLLYWOOD

SOUTH AMERICA

PACIFIC OCEAN

The Royal Yacht Britannia

DID YOU KNOW?

THERE HAVE BEEN THREE ASSASSINATION ATTEMPTS ON THE LIFE OF THE QUEEN DURING HER REIGN. THE MOST SERIOUS WAS IN 1981 DURING 'TROOPING THE COLOUR' WHEN A MAN FIRED AT THE QUEEN AFTER BEING INSPIRED BY THE 1980 SHOOTING OF BEATLE JOHN LENNON.

'BURMESE' THE QUEEN'S HORSE

THE QUEEN MADE HER FIRST CHRISTMAS DAY SPEECH IN 1952. 2022 WILL BE HER 70TH CHRISTMAS DAY MESSAGE TO THE NATION.

AS WELL AS HER FAMOUS CORGIS, THE QUEEN OWNS AN ELEPHANT, TWO GIANT TORTOISES, A JAGUAR, AND TWO SLOTHS.

THE QUEEN FIRST SENT AN EMAIL IN 1976....
AND PUBLISHED HER FIRST INSTAGRAM
POST IN 2019.

QUEEN ELIZABETH II IS THE
LONGEST REIGNING MONARCH
EVER IN BRITAIN, BEATING EVEN
QUEEN VICTORIA, HER GREAT-
GREAT- GRANDMA!

THE QUEEN'S NICKNAMES INCLUDE "LILIBET"
AND "CABBAGE." SHE GOT THE NICKNAME
"LILIBET" WHEN SHE WAS YOUNG AND COULDN'T
PRONOUNCE HER NAME. KING GEORGE VI USED
TO TALK ABOUT HIS DAUGHTERS, SAYING,
"LILIBET IS MY PRIDE, AND MARGARET IS MY JOY"
IT HAS ALSO BEEN REPORTED THAT PRINCE PHILIP
LOVINGLY REFERRED TO HIS WIFE AS "CABBAGE."

THE QUEEN IS THE ONLY PERSON IN THE
UK ALLOWED TO DRIVE WITHOUT A LICENCE.

THE QUEEN HAS TWO BIRTHDAYS - HER REAL ONE - ON 21 APRIL, AS SHE WAS BORN ON 21 APRIL 1926 AND TURNED 96 THIS YEAR. THEN A SECOND ONE - THE OFFICIAL CELEBRATION - ON THE SECOND SATURDAY OF JUNE.

QUEEN ELIZABETH HAS SENT OVER 50,000 CHRISTMAS CARDS DURING HER REIGN, THAT'S A LOT OF STAMPS!

RICHARD GRIFFIN, WHO WORKED PROTECTING THE ROYALS FOR YEARS, TOLD A RATHER CHARMING STORY ABOUT WALKING WITH HER AT BALMORAL, HER SUMMER RESIDENCE. SHE WAS WEARING EVERYDAY CLOTHES - A MACINTOSH AND A SCARF, HE SAID. SO WHEN A GROUP OF AMERICAN TOURISTS STOPPED FOR A CHAT, THEY HAD NO IDEA WHO SHE WAS. WHEN ONE OF THEM ASKED, "DO YOU LIVE AROUND HERE?", SHE WENT ALONG WITH IT, SAYING THAT SHE HAD A HOUSE NEARBY. THEY ASKED IF SHE HAD EVER MET THE QUEEN. TRUTHFULLY, SHE REPLIED, "NO, BUT HE HAS", GESTURING TO HER PROTECTION OFFICER.

70

Her Royal Highness

Her Majesty, Queen Elizabeth

ENGLAND

SCOTLAND

IRELAND

WALES

WOOF!

Dookie

WOOF!

Susan

Queen Elizabeth II

1952   2022

LILY OF THE VALLEY –
HER MAJESTY'S FAVOURITE FLOWER

MONTY

WILLOW

THE ROYAL CORGIS
Holly Bushnell Illustration

A page from the Queen's Scrapbook

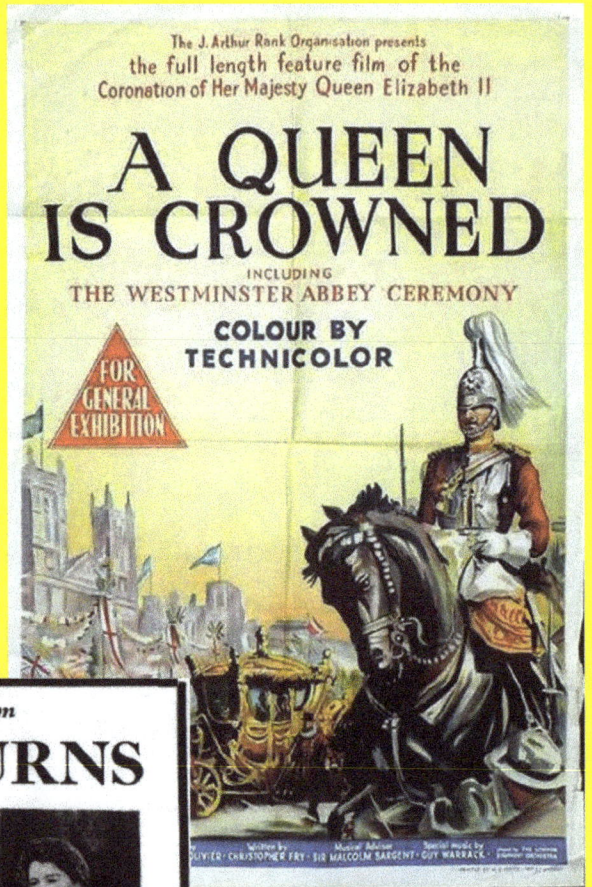

3D AUSTRALIA

The J. Arthur Rank Organisation presents
the full length feature film of the Coronation of Her Majesty Queen Elizabeth II

A QUEEN IS CROWNED

INCLUDING
THE WESTMINSTER ABBEY CEREMONY

COLOUR BY TECHNICOLOR

FOR GENERAL EXHIBITION

Written by OLIVIER · CHRISTOPHER FRY · SIR MALCOLM SARGENT · GUY WARRACK

1d. POSTAGE REVENUE 1d.

POSTAGE REVENUE FIVE PENCE

POSTAGE REVENUE 8d.

Passed Away Peacefully in His Sleep at Sandringham

WHOLE NATION MOURNS THE KING'S DEATH

New Queen Flying Back At Once From Africa

PRINCESS ELIZABETH, who a week ago waved from her aircraft at London Airport to her father, King George the Sixth, standing bareheaded to wish his daughter Godspeed on her journey to Africa, is to-day flying back to England as Queen. To-night she will be proclaimed Sovereign.

At 10.45 this morning the whole nation and Empire was stunned by the announcement that the King, who retired to rest last night in his usual health, had passed peacefully away in his sleep early this morning. He was in his 57th year, and the 16th year...

...four months after his...

...tion.

...at Sandringham, though...

...se grounds near the big...

...George V, also died...

...21, 1936.

Theatres...

Cine...

Cl...

THE NEW QUEEN

The Last Time

The last time the public saw the King was at London Airport on Thursday, when at 11.44 a.m., 3,000 people watched him arrive with the Queen and Princess Margaret to bid farewell to Princess Elizabeth and the Duke of Edinburgh as they left for their Commonwealth tour.

...well and cheer...

...ugh he wore...

...not to...

...and...

...as...

COMMONS' SORROW

AS soon as the Speaker had taken his seat in the Commons this afternoon at 2.45, Mr. Churchill slowly rose and said, "The House will have learned with deep sorrow of the death of His Majesty King George VI.

"We cannot at this moment do more than record a spontaneous expression of our grief.

"The...

ELIZABETH·II·DEI·GRA·BRITT·OMN·REGINA·F:D

Coronation year coins

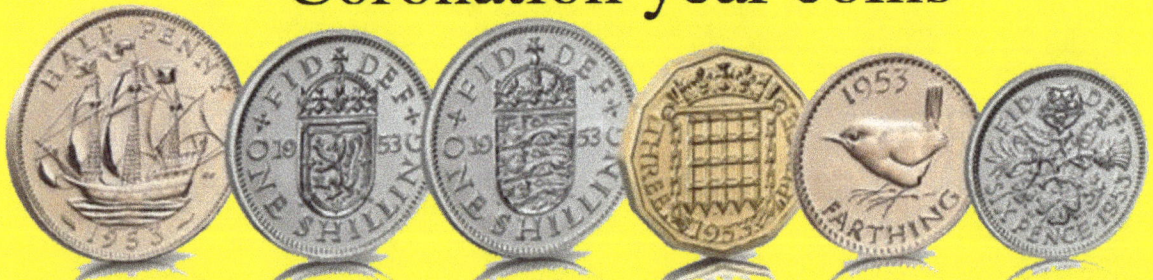